I LOVE ISLAM

WORKBOOK

3

Ahmed Sahbani

ISLAMIC STUDIES TEXTBOOK SERIES   **LEVEL 3**

I Love Islam © is a series of Islamic Studies textbooks that gradually introduces Muslim students to the essentials of their faith. It brings to light the historic and cultural aspects of Islam. The series covers levels one through five, which are suitable for young learners and includes a student textbooks and workbooks as well as a teacher and parent's guides.

The Islamic Services Foundation is undertaking this project in collaboration with Brighter Horizons Academy in Dallas, Texas. Extensive efforts have been made to review the enclosed material; However, constructive suggestions and comments that would enrich the content of this work are welcome.

All praise is due to Allah (God), for providing us with the resources that have enabled us to complete the first part of this series. This is an ongoing project, and it is our sincere wish and hope that it will impact our Muslim children today, and for many years to come.

PUBLISHER AND OWNER:

 **ISF** PUBLICATIONS

Islamic Services Foundation
P.O. Box 451623
Garland, Texas 75045
U.S.A
Tel: +1 972-414-5090
Fax: +1 972-414-5640
www.myislamicbooks.com

Workbook prepared by:

Neha Firoze
Maryam Syed

UNIT A

Exercise 1

Directions: Circle "Islam" if the action is a pillar of Islam.
Circle "Iman" if the action is a pillar of Iman.
Circle "Neither" if the action is not a pillar of Islam or Iman.

1- Shahadah	Islam	Iman	Neither	1- Sunnah	Islam	Iman	Neither
2- Prophets	Islam	Iman	Neither	2- Umrah	Islam	Iman	Neither
3- Al-Qadar	Islam	Iman	Neither	3- Zakah	Islam	Iman	Neither
4- Siyam	Islam	Iman	Neither	4- Books	Islam	Iman	Neither
5-Hajj	Islam	Iman	Neither	5-Angels	Islam	Iman	Neither
6-Day of Judgment	Islam	Iman	Neither	6-Quran	Islam	Iman	Neither

Exercise 2

Directions: Fill in the blanks the six pillars of Iman

IMAN IS THE HEART OF ISLAM

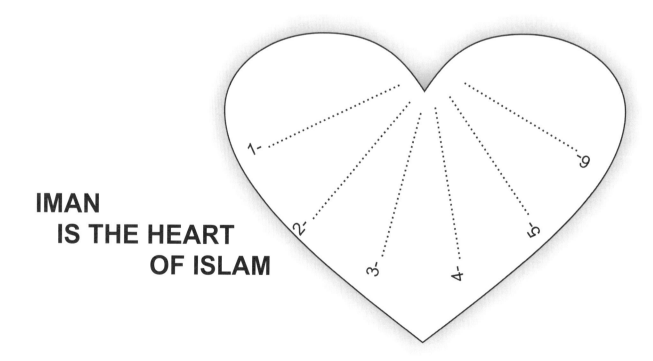

Exercise 3

Directions: Match the pillars to their correct pairs.

Exercise 4

Directions: Calegorize the words from the "Word List" into either circles.

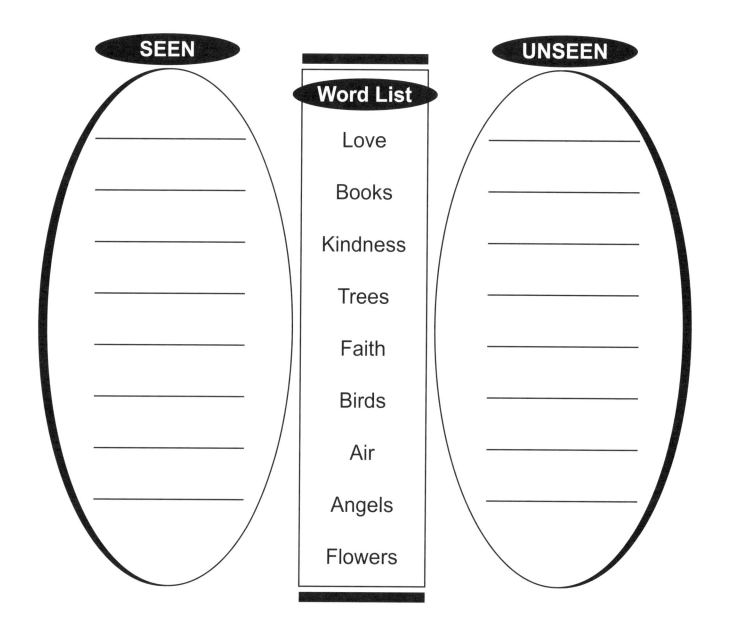

SEEN

Word List

Love

Books

Kindness

Trees

Faith

Birds

Air

Angels

Flowers

UNSEEN

Exercise 1

Directions: Zaid is writing a report about Allah (SWT), He needs to complete this lest paragraph, Help him out by looking at some clues from Zaid "Clue Book."

Allah made ....¹... . He also made ...²...

in the ....³... .

He also created the strong ....⁴... .

He created everything, and He is ....⁵... . 1

MORE CLUES

1- This word starts with the letter P.

2- This word ends with the sound "sshhh!."

3- This word rhymes with "bee."

4- This word reminds you of big "mounts."

5- this word reminds you of the 1st pillar of Iman discussed in this chapter.

Up, Up, and Away!

Exercise 2

Directions: Insha-Allah, we will all get to see Allah (SWT) in the Heavens. Let's begin our way there by answering the questions below. Write each answer on the blank stairs leading upwards.

1- What are Allah's names called in Arabic?

2- Is it wrong to worship more than one God?

3- Is Al-Azeez one of the names of Allah?

4- How many names does Allah have?

5- Did Allah create us humans because He wanted us to worship Satan?

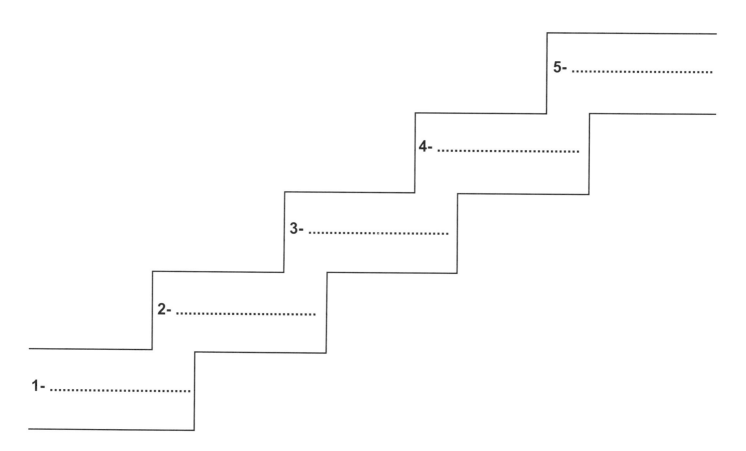

Exercise 3

Directions: Answer the question below. Cross out the sins a person loses and trace the rewards when a person gains ajr.

1- If Ali said the hadeeth two times, how would his sins and rewards change? Cross out the sins and trace the rewards he gains.

2- If Ali said the hadeeth one time the next morning, how would his sins and rewards change? Cross out the sins and trace the rewards he gains.

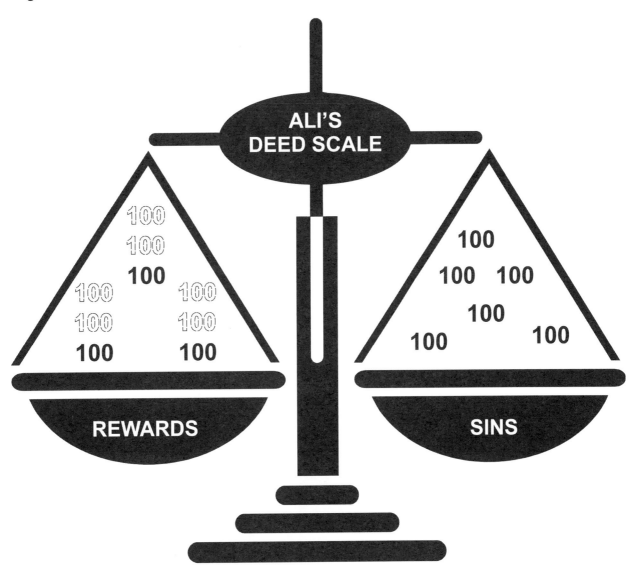

Exercise 1

Directions: Complete the profiles below

The Angels

Name of Angel: Jibreel..................
Job of Angel: ....
....
....
....
....

Name of Angel: ....
Job of Angel: Takes special care
of rain..
....
....
....

Name of Angel: Israfeel.................
Job of Angel: ....
....
....
....
....

Name of Angel: Ridwan...............
Job of Angel: ....
....
....
....
....

Name of Angel: ....
Job of Angel: The guardian of
hellfire ....
....
....
....

Name of Angel: Angel of Death
Job of Angel: ....
....
....
....
....

Exercise 2

Directions: Read the story below, write Mohammad's good deeds on his right angel and his bad deeds on his left angel.

"Mohammad, wake up for Fajr," his mom said. Mohammad looked at his clock and went back to sleep. A few hours passed, and Mahammad's mom woke him up to eat breakfast. He brushed and went downstairs to eat. He said his du'aa' first and obeyed his mom's order of washing the dishes every morning. He then got ready for school. On his way out, he dropped his mom's favorite vase, looked at it, and ran off.

Right Angel   **Left Angel**

Exercise 3

Directions: Match each description to its correct pair.

Angels

الحفظة

Al-Ka'bah

One Angel

Malak

Amazing
Creations

The Guardian
Angels

Al Bayt
Al-Ma'mour

Exercise 1

Directions: The Qur'an is our guide. It directs us when we need help and are lost or confused. Find your way to the majid by answering the questions below. Follow the arrows under each correct answer. If true, color in the arrow under true. If false, color in the arrow under false.

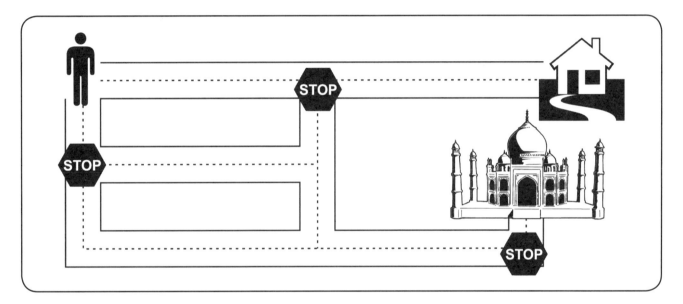

1- Al Qur'an has 14 suwar, or chapters.

2- Az-Zaboor was revealed to Prophet Dawood (PBUH)

3- Al-Injeel was revealed to Prophet Musa (PBUH)

4- As-Suhuf have been lost.

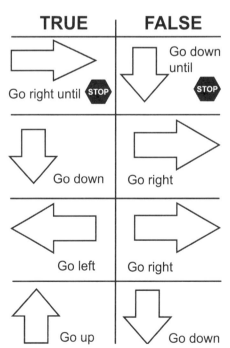

TRUE	FALSE
Go right until STOP	Go down until STOP
Go down	Go right
Go left	Go right
Go up	Go down

Exercise 2

Directions: Look at the word bank below. Than, fill in the blanks until the message reaches it people. You can use the words in the words box more than once.

WORD BANK
Prophets **-** Allah **-** Angel Jibreel **-** People

From:

....

....

  To:

  ....

  ....

Place
Stamp
Here

From:

....

....

  To:

  ....

  ....

Place
Stamp
Here

From:

....

....

  To:

  ....

  ....

Place
Stamp
Here

Exercise 3

Directions: Copy this paragraph in the farme's lines below.

"Allah (SWT) taught Al-Qur'an to Muhammad (P). Muslims copied the entire Qur'an down and memorized it by heart before the Prophet passed away. After the passing of Prophet Muhammad (P) Muslims made many copies of it and kept them in masajid, homes, and schools."

```
........................................................................
........................................................................
........................................................................
........................................................................
........................................................................
........................................................................
........................................................................
........................................................................
........................................................................
```

Now, find a partner and try to recite the paragraph to him / her without looking back. This will test your memorization!

Exercise 1

Directions: It's time you create your own test! Let's pretend you are the teacher like the prophets were teachers to their people. Remember, every prophet spoke the language of his people, use the decoder below to complete the question and answers.

A-1	B-2	C-3	D-4	E-5	F-6	G-7	H-8	I-9	J-10	K-11	L-12
M-13	N-14	O-15	P-16	Q-17	R-18	S-19	T-20	U-21	V-22	W-23	X-24
				Y-25	Z-26						

1- What is the Arabic word for .... ?
 16   18   15   16   8   5   20   19

Answer: .... or Rasool
 14   1   2   9   25   25

2- How many prophets did Allah mention in the .... ?
 17   21   18   1   14

Answer: ....
 20   23   5   14   20   25   6   9   22   5

3- Why did .... send prophets to people ?
 1   12   12   1   8

Answer: ....
 20   15   20   5   1   3   8   20   8   5   13

 ....
 9   19   12   1   13

 **Exercise 2**

Directions: Complete the left circle by writing down prophets who were mentioned in the Holy Qur'an. In the right circle, there are names of Allah's books. In the middle circle, write down the names of prophets who also received the books of Allah. We also call them massengers.

Prophets of Allah   Books of Allah

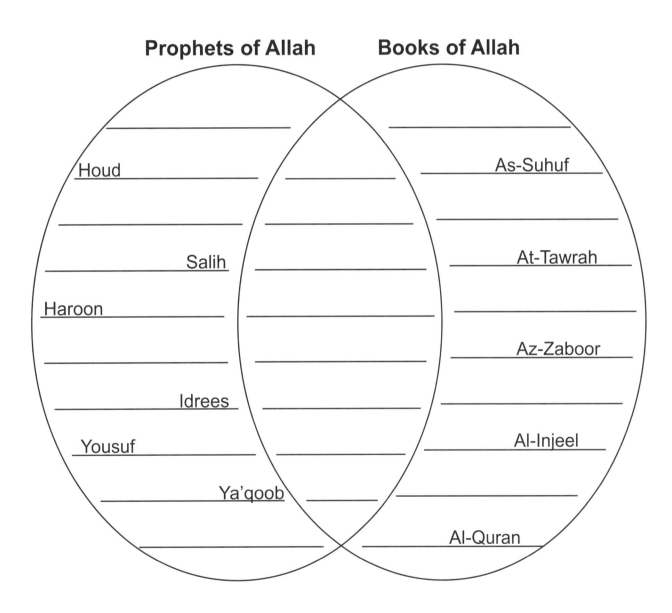

Houd

Salih

Haroon

Idrees

Yousuf

Ya'qoob

As-Suhuf

At-Tawrah

Az-Zaboor

Al-Injeel

Al-Quran

Exercise 3

Directions: Zaid wanted to write Hassan a letter about the prophets of Allah. Fill in the blanks with words from the Word Box. You do not have to use all the words in the Word Box.

Word Box		
Obey	Twenty-Two	Qur'an
Ishaq	Prophets	People
Isa	Animals	Bible
Omar	Twenty-five	Muslims

Dear Hassan,

Did you know that Allah (SWT) has mentioned ....

prophets in our ....? These prophets are sent to teach

us how to live as good .... Prophets wanted to remind

us to .... God's rules. Some names of our prophets

are ...., ..., and Muhammad

(peace be on them). Do you want to know more Hassan? Prophet

Muhammad (P) said: "Prophets are the best of all ...."

Your friend,

Zaid

18

Exercise 4

Directions: Out of all prophets mentioned in the chapter, pick a prophet and find out more about him.

The Prophets

Prophet Name:

....

Did he own a book of Allah? ....

Married or Single? ....

Did he have kids? ....

If yes, how many? ....

Mention a story of him: ....

....

....

....

....

Exercise 1

Directions: Complete this maze by following the "FORGIVEN" and not falling into the trap of being "not forgiven".

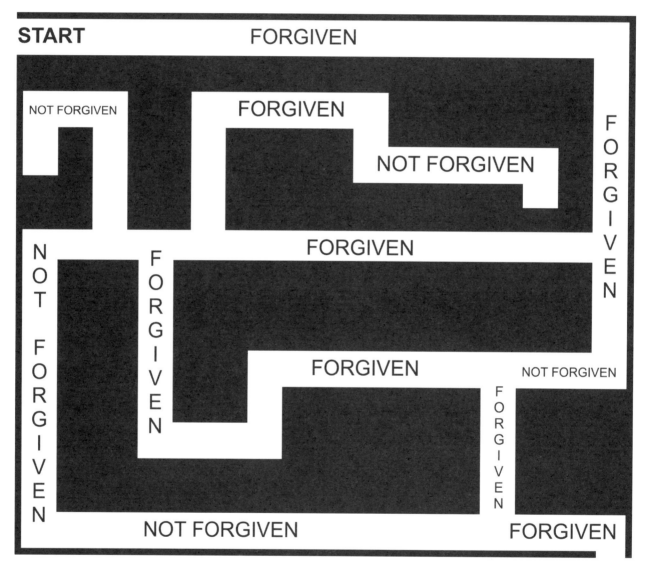

START

FORGIVEN

NOT FORGIVEN

FORGIVEN

NOT FORGIVEN

FORGIVEN

FORGIVEN

NOT FORGIVEN

FORGIVEN

NOT FORGIVEN

FORGIVEN

FORGIVEN

NOT FORGIVEN

FORGIVEN

Exercise 2

Directions: Cut each hand and color the right with green and the left with red. Then, find a partner and tell him/her to recite the sentences below. If the action is a bad deed, raise the left hand. If it is a good deed, raise the right hand. Then you may switch positions and let your partner give it a try!

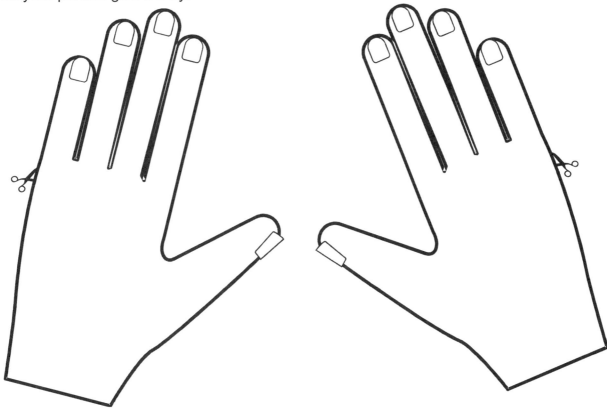

Actions: Good or Bad?

- Missing Fajr prayer in the morning.
- Fasting in Ramadan.
- Helping the poor.
- Lying to your parents.
- Stealing chocolates from your sister/brother.
- Disobeying your parents.

It's Raining, It's Pouring!

Exercise 1

Directions: Read the story below. Than, answer the questions in complete sentences.

Ahmad and Zaid were playing basketball. The audience cheered for both teams. It was getting cloudy and dark as the game continued. As Zaid was dribbling the ball, he felt a drop of rain on his nose. Suddenly, someone screamed, "It's raining!" The score was a tie, and the game had to end because of the bad weather. No one won the game, and everyone went home.

1- Although this story has a sad ending, there may be some good added in Mention three good things that came out from this sad-ending story.

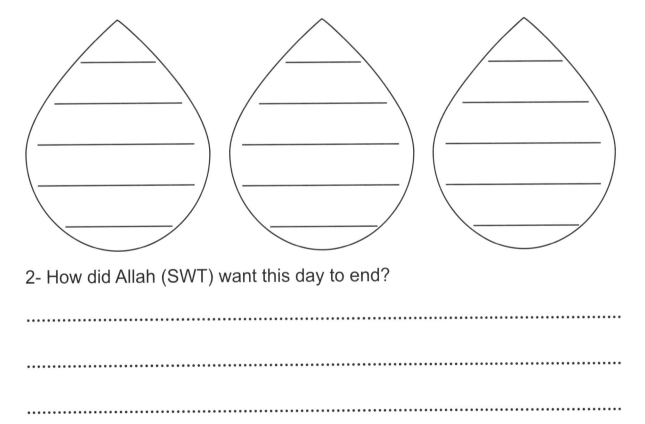

2- How did Allah (SWT) want this day to end?

....

....

....

Exercise 2

Directions: Read the three situations below. Place a check in the correct box and state why you think this is the correct answer.

1- **Zaid:** Mama, will I be rich when I grow up?
Mama: I hope you will Zaid. What will you do with all that money?
Zaid: I am going to help the poor and make them rich too!
Mama: (laughs) Insha'allah Zaid.

This situation deals with:
☐ Al-Ajal   ☐ As-Sihhah   ☐ Ar-Rizq   ☐ Life Quality
because ....

2- **Zaid:** Mama, I missed school today too! When will I get better?
Mama: Zaid, we must be patient and say "Alhamdulillah." You should be thankful that you are not sick with something worse. Now say istighfar.
Zaid: Ok, sorry Mama.

This situation deals with:
☐ Al-Ajal   ☐ As-Sihhah   ☐ Ar-Rizq   ☐ Life Quality
because..

3- Mama: Zaid, do you know what happened today?
Zaid: Mama, what's wrong? What happened?
Mam: Our close friend, Ahmed, passed away today.
Zaid: Oh Mama, that scares me. I don't want to think about when my turn will come.
Mama: Only Allah (SWT) knows. May Allah give you a blessed life.

This situation deals with:
☐ Al-Ajal   ☐ As-Sihhah   ☐ Ar-Rizq   ☐ Life Quality
because..

UNIT B

Exercise 1

Directions: Prophet Ibraheem was seasching for Allah (SWT). In this exercise, search for the completions of the sentences and write them in the lines provided. Make sure the sentences make sense. You can solve this puzzle by matching an item from part A to another in part B.

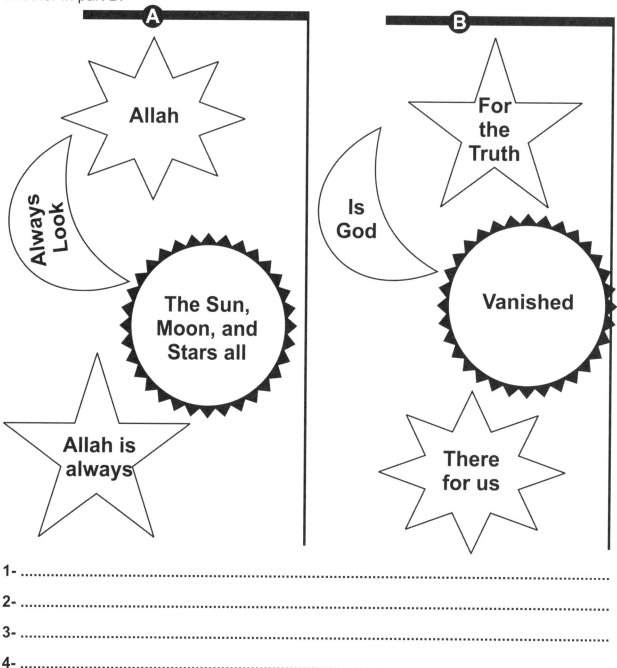

1- ....

2- ....

3- ....

4- ....

Exercise 2

Directions: Read each sentence below. Mark it TRUE or FALSE, If FALSE, correct the statement.

1- Ibraheem (P) never believed in Allah (SWT) ....

Correction: ....

....

....

2- Allah ordered Ibraheem (P) to do something unusual. ....

Correction: ....

....

....

3- Allah could not bring the four birds back to life. ....

Correction: ....

....

....

4- Prophet Ibraheem was amazed when he saw the live birds. ....

Correction: ....

....

....

Exercise 1

Directions: The moral of Prophet Ibraheem's story is to tell the truth. Read the story below, and complete its ending by writing what you think is the best thing Zaid should say.

Zaid was sitting on a swing in his school's playground. The school had just planted a new plant in front of the swings. Zaid looked at it with amazement because it was so beautiful. Suddenly, he saw two boys laughing and coming towards the plant. They looked at it, and both stepped on it at the same time. They began giggling and one said to the other, "Come on, let's go!" Zaid saw it all happen and was shocked. After a few minutes, a teacher passed by with the two boys by her side and asked them, "Are you sure you boys did not destory this?" They said, "No, teacher." The teatcher then turned to Zaid and asked, "Zaid, you were on those swings for quite a while. Did you see anything?" Zaid took a deep breath and said, "..............

....

....

....

....

....

....

 ## Exercise 2

Directions: Ibraheem (P) tried to convince people that Allah (SWT) was their God, and idols could never take His place, But, the people did not listen to him. Can you think of things that Allah can easily do but idols can never do? Write them down in the lines below.

IDOLS CANNOT	ALLAH CAN
1-	1- ....
2-	2- ....
3-	3- ....
4-	4- ....
5-	5- ....
6-	6- ....

Exercise 1

Directions: Write these events in their correct order.

▶ King Numrude ordered his guards to bring two people from the prison who deserved to die.

▶ King Numrude ordered his soldiers to find Prophet Ibraheem.

▶ King Numrude ordered his soldiers to burn Ibraheem alive.

▶ Allah سبحانه وتعالى saved Prophet Ibraheem عليه السلام , and he moved with others to Palestine.

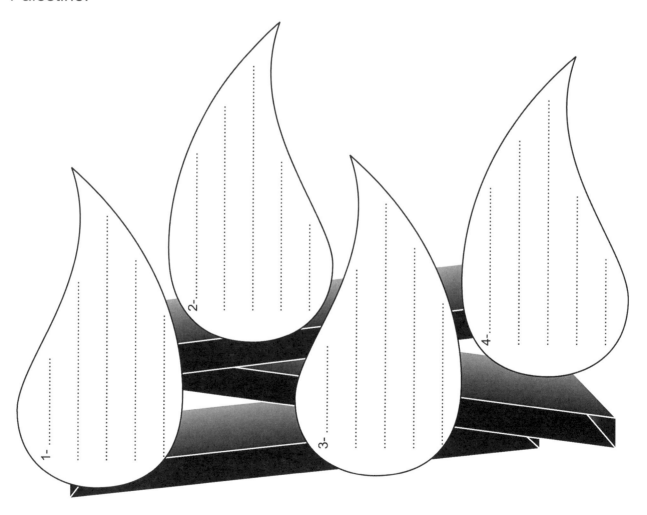

TRUST-O-METER

Exercise 2

Directions: This chapter teaches us to have trust in Allah (SWT). Read each story below. Circle "trust" if you think the story displays one's trust in Allah (SWT). Circle "no trust" if you think the story displays no trust in Allah (SWT).

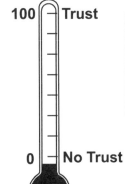

Zaid and his friends were watching a movie about Islamic history. They saw a scene where Muslim soldiers were a few in number and were still ready to fight with several more enemy soldiers.

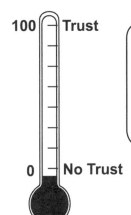

Zaid heard about a stampede of people during Hajj. He told himself he didn't want to make Hajj because he was scared. He forgot that Hajj was a command from Allah سبحانه وتعالى .

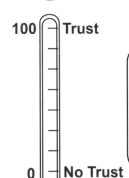

A Muslim girl was being threatened by some bad people. They kept bothering her at school and made fun of her hijab. But the girl didn't care because she knew she was pleasing Allah سبحانه وتعالى .

Exercise 3

Directions: Verbs are words that describe action(S). In the paragraph below, underline the verb(s) and verb phrases and write them in the blank lines.

When king Numrude brought Prophet Ibraheem عليه السلام in front of him, the prophet told him about Allah سبحانه وتعالى :

> "My Lord cerated me and He guides me. He give me food and drink. When I am ill He cures me. He is the only one who can make me die, and then bring me back to life."

In the blanks below, write down all the verbs and verb phrases in the paragraph above. These will remind you of everything Allah (SWT) has done for you.

Allah ....

Allah ....

Allah ....

Allah ....

Allah .... (Verb phrase)

Allah .... (Verb phrase)

Exercise 1

Directions: Look at each picture, Use your imagination, and write a sentences that describes each picture. Than, find a partner and compare your sentences with each other

Family Tree

Ibraheem ⟷ Hager

Isma'eel

Al-Marwah

As-Safa

Makkah Before

Makkah After

Sentence #1 ....

....

....

....

....

....

....

Sentence #2 ....

....

....

....

....

....

....

Sentence #3 ....

....

....

....

....

....

....

Exercise 2

Directions: Read each word in the droplets of water. Than, make a sentence that has that word in it. Be creative!

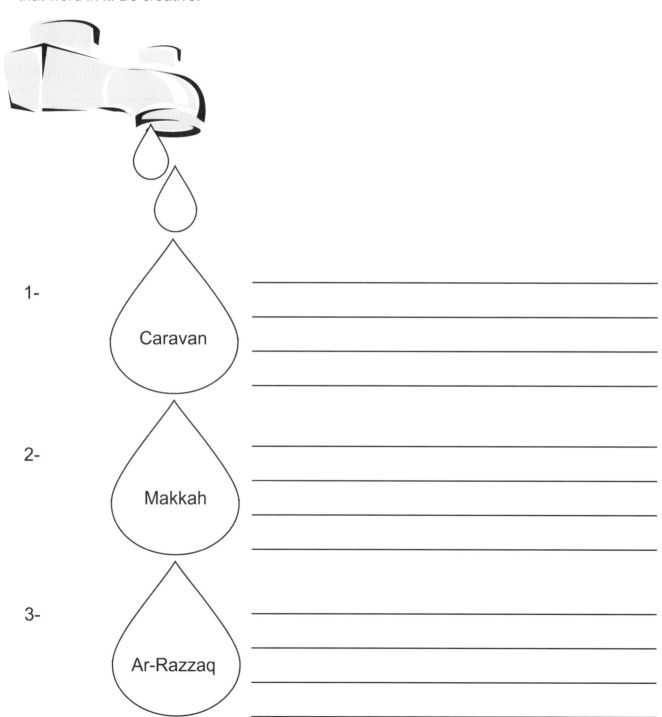

1- Caravan _____

2- Makkah _____

3- Ar-Razzaq _____

Exercise 3

Directions: Allah (SWT) tested Prophet Ibraheem in many ways because he was such a great believer, he passed every test. Read each test below. Let's pretend you are the teacher now and you have to put a grade on each test. If you think the person passed Allah's (SWT) test, write an "A" in the blank. If you think the person failed Allah's (SWT) test, write an "F" in the blank.

Test Grade:................

Leena won a contest, and her prize was 50 dollars! She is so happy because she can buy some toys for herself. However, she first decides to share her money with the poor and give sadaqah/ charity. She remembers that giving ssdaqah is one of the things that lead to Jannah.

Test Grade:................

Allah (SWT) commands us to fast in Ramadan. Osama does not have enough patience to fast and ends up eating his favorite candy. He breaks his fast and does not have enough patience.

Test Grade: ....

Adam's favorite TV program is coming on. His mom comes in the room to remind him to pray Asr prayer. Mohammad does not want to miss his favorite show so he continues watching it. It finishes and so does the time for prayer. He has missed his Asr prayer instead of missing his TV program!

Exercise 4

Directions: What is the spring called? Trace the maze by following the numbers and than write it down. Color the words in.

Start

Finish

UNIT B
Chapter 5

Exercise 1

Directions: Read each statement below. Color in Ibraheem's (PBUH) footsteps depending on each answer. For example, if the answer to number 5 is true, then color the footstep marked "5, TRUE." Have fun! Color the (true)s in green and the (false)s in red.

1- Ibraheem عليه السلام had a disturbing dream of killing his only son Ishaq.

2- Prophet Ibraheem had to choose between his love for Allah and his son.

3- When Ibraheem عليه السلام told his son about the vision, his son was very patient.

4- Iblees was happy to see Ibraheem and his son obeying Allah's سبحانه وتعالى commands.

5- Mina is a place near Madinah.

6- Prophet Ibraheem did not win the love of Allah سبحانه وتعالى .

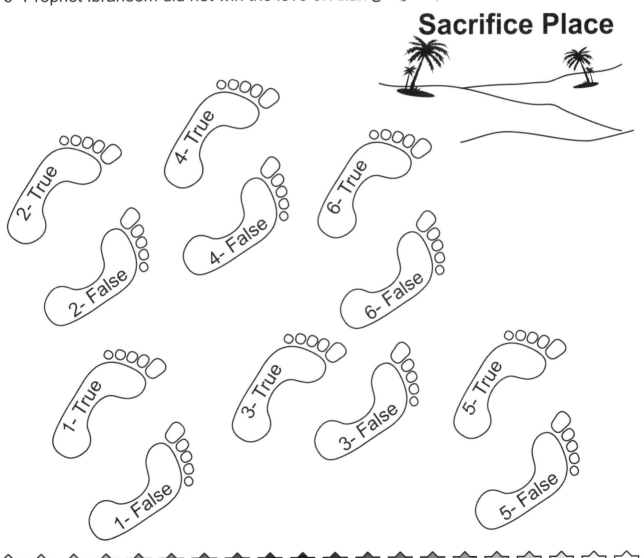

Sacrifice Place

2- True

2- False

4- True

4- False

6- True

6- False

1- True

1- False

3- True

3- False

5- True

5- False

37

Exercise 2

Directions: Match each hint to its correct number.

This number is how many times Ibraheem عليه السلام had his vision to sacrifice his only son, Isma'eel

This number is how old Isma'eel was when Ibraheem عليه السلام approached him with his vision.

This is how many miles Palestine is far away from Makkah.

This is how many years Prophet Ibraheem was separated from Hager and Isma'eel in Makkah.

This is how old Ibraheem عليه السلام was when he Traveled from Palestine to Makkah.

12

3

100

12

800

Exercise 3

Directions: The Prophet Ibraheem عليه السلام threw stones at Satan. Can you tell which of These stones will hit Satan? Circle the stone(s).

Exercise 1

Directions: Allah ordered the Prophet Ibraheem عليه السلام to clean the Ka'bah for those who came there to pray and to call all people to make the pilgrimage.
Can you help these pilgrims who have come in a caravan and on a ship to reach Makkah?

 **Exercise 2**

<u>Directions</u>: Fill in the blanks with words from the word box. You do not have to use all the words in the box.

Word Box

Al-Hajar-ul-Aswad
Maqamu Ibraheem
Al-Ka'bah
Al-Hajj
Prophet Muhammad (P)
Prophet Ibraheem (P)

1- The first masjid is known as .... It literally means the cubic building.

2- .... is a white stone that came from Jannah. Later, this white stone became black because of the many sins the people did.

3- When Muslims travel to Makkah to make a pilgrimage, they are performing an act called ....

4- The place where Ibraheem stood and made the call for Al-Hajj is called

....

5- Allah سبحانه وتعالى answered Ibraheem's prayers by making ....

His Messenger.

UNIT C

Exercise 1

Directions: Fill in the blanks to complete the paragraph. Then, use the letter in each shape to answer the question at the bottom.

Hajj is a ☐ __ __ __ on every adult Muslim if he or she is in

good ♡__ __ __○♡ and can __☐△ __ __ __ it. This happens in

the month of ○♡__ __ ♡△__ __ __ . This means the month

of ♡__ __ __ . It is the __ __ __ __ __○♡ month of the lunar year.

What pillar of Islam is Hajj?

☐△☐○♡

Exercise 2

Directions: Draw arrows towards each step (and number them). You might have to go to the same place twice.

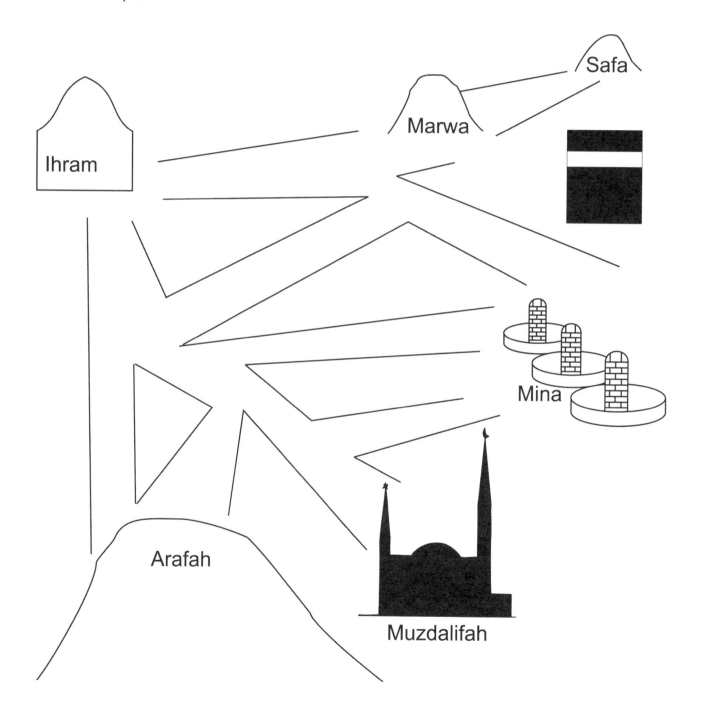

Ihram

Marwa

Safa

Mina

Arafah

Muzdalifah

Exercise 3

Directions: For each of the following steps, write down what it reminds us of in the memory bubble. The first one is completed for you.

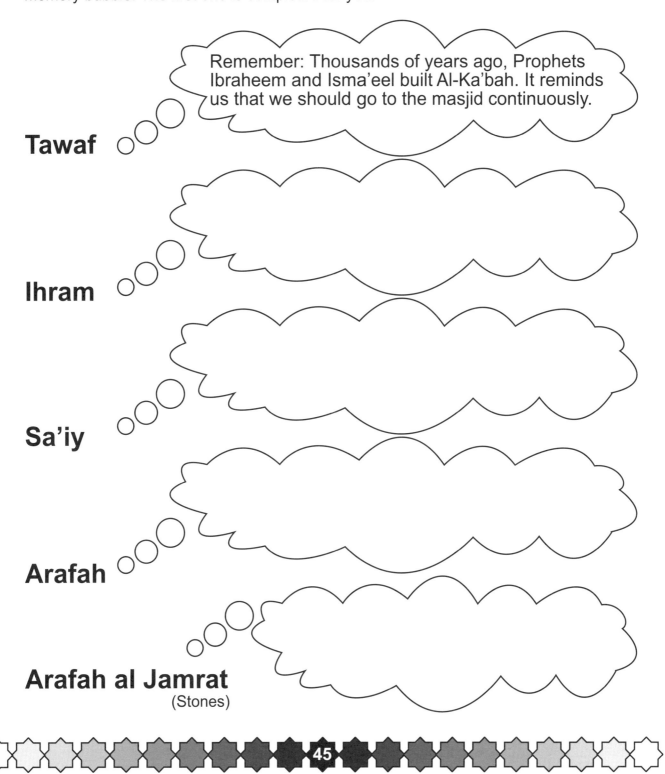

Tawaf

Remember: Thousands of years ago, Prophets Ibraheem and Isma'eel built Al-Ka'bah. It reminds us that we should go to the masjid continuously.

Ihram

Sa'iy

Arafah

Arafah al Jamrat
(Stones)

Exercise 1

Directions: Read each situation and put yourself in that position. What would be the best thing to do?

It is almost Maghrib time and you and your friend rush to the bathroom to make wudoo'. You see an elder person not making wudoo' the right way. What would you do?

- -

- -

- -

- -

You wake your little brother for Fajr prayer. He stands up immediately and gets ready for the Takbir. What do you say to him?

- -

- -

- -

- -

You and your friends are bored. One friend decides to try something new and begins making wudoo' with her apple juice! What do you say to them?

- -

- -

- -

- -

Exercise 2

<u>**Directions**</u>: Number the body parts in order that you wash them during wudoo' starting with the hands. Then, color what parts of the body will have a shining light in the Day of Judgment if you perform wudoo' correctly.

Exercise 3

Directions: Put a check in the proper category to show how many times each step is preformed.

Steps of doing wudoo'	1 one time	3 three times
1. Niyyah and saying "bismillah"		
2. Washing Hands		
3. Washing Mouth		
4. Washing Nose		
5. Washing Face		
6. Washing Arms		
7. Wiping Head		
8. Cleaning Ears		
9. Washing Feet		
10. Saying Shahadah and Du'aa'		

Exercise 4

Directions: Answer each question. Then, write the number of the question according to the order of true answer, from least to greatest.

1. Number of gates open for the person who does wudoo': _____

2. Number of steps of wudoo': _____

3. Number of ways to break wudoo': _____

4. Number of Prophet's grandsons who helped their elder in making wudoo': _____

5. Number of times you clean your ear in wudoo': _____

Question_ < Question_ < Question_ < Question_ < Question_

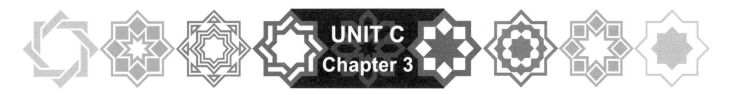
Exercise 1

Directions: Write down the connection between the two people below. An example is done for you.

Abdullah Ibn Um Maktoom mua'thin of the Rasoolullah

Abdullah Ibn
Um Maktoom

of Madinah when the Prophet was traveling

Abdullah Ibn Abbas

of Maymoonah

Abdullah Ibn Abbas

of the Rasoolullah

Exercise 2

Directions: Fill in the number that completes each of the following. Then, fill in the answers according to their order to find the final number.

1. Salah in the jama'ah is .... times better than praying alone.

2. The Prophet (PBUH) and Abdullah Ibn Abbas prayed .... rak'aat together for Qiyam.

3. One must stand to the right of the imam if there are only .... people doing Salatul'Jama'ah.

4. We Pray Salat-ul-Jama'ah .... time a week

Exercise 3

Directions: The Prophet (PBUH) was very wise. So we have to understand why he made his decisions. Read each of the Prophet's actions and explain why each was the best decision.

> Although the man was blind, Allah wanted him to come to the masjid everyday. Why?

_____
_____
_____

> The Prophet (PBUH) would get angry with those who were often absent in Salat-ul-Juma'ah without good reasons. Why?

_____
_____
_____

> Abdullah Ibn Abbas joined the Prophet (PBUH) when he saw him praying "Qiyam-ul-layl." Why?

_____
_____
_____

Exercise 1

Directions: Fill out the chart by writing what a follower in Salat-ul-Jama'ah would do. An example has been done.

Imam	Ma'moom
Says "Allahu Akbar" loudly.	Says "Allahu Akbar" silently.
Read Qur'an loudly (In Fajr, Maghrib, and Isha)	
Reading Qur'an silently (In Thuhr and Asr)	
Makes rukoo'	
Says "Subhana Rabbiya Al-Atheem" silently during rukoo'	
Says "Sami' Allahu liman hamidah" loudly after rukoo'	
Stays silently "Rabbana Walak Al-Hamd' during stand-up after rukoo'	
Making sujood	
Saying "Subhana Rabiyal Ala" silently during Sujood	
Says tasleem loudly	

Exercise 2

Directions: Look at each picture of the imam. Draw the Muslim that is on the side of the box where he or she should be standing in the prayer.

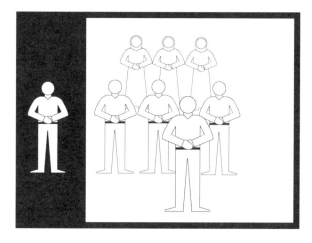

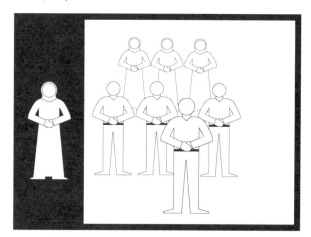

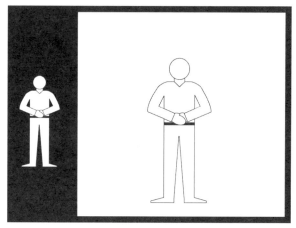

 Exercise 3

<u>Directions</u>: Pretend you are a detective. You have to find out what "Salatul-Jama'ah" is and answer the five W's : Who? What? Where? When? Why?

Who: ....
....
....
What: ....
....
....
Where: ....
....
....
When: ....
....
....
Why: ....
....
....

 ## Exercise 1

Directions: Write down what each saying refers to, both in English and Arabic.

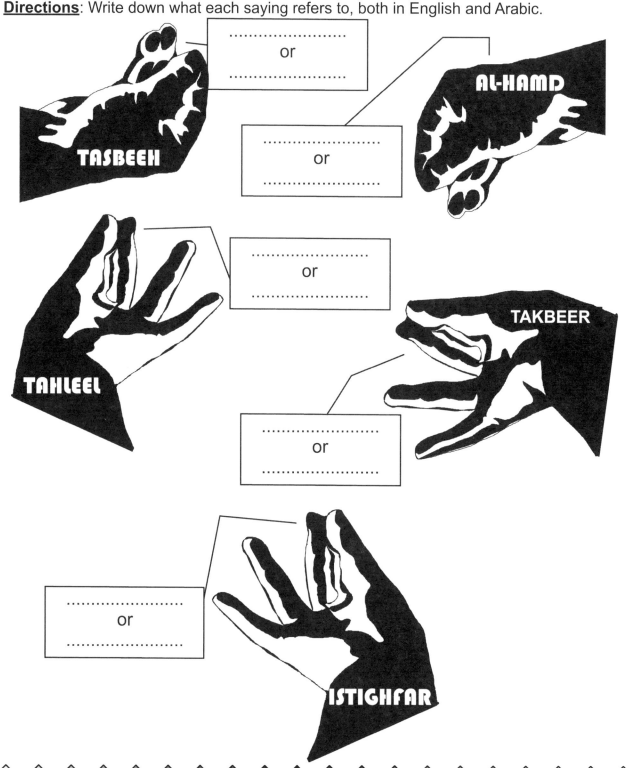

Exercise 2

<u>Directions</u>: Read each situation and put yourself in that position. What you you say?

You win a contest ➡️ ....

Face a challenge ➡️ ....

You miss Fajr prayer ➡️ ....

You hear the name of
the Prophet ➡️ ....

You are happy ➡️ ....

You are angry ➡️ ....

You are mean to
your sister / brother ➡️ ....

Before you read the
Qur'an ➡️ ....

Exercise 3

Directions: You have a mission. Shaytan has tied 3 knots behind your head. Write down what you would do to help untie each kont.

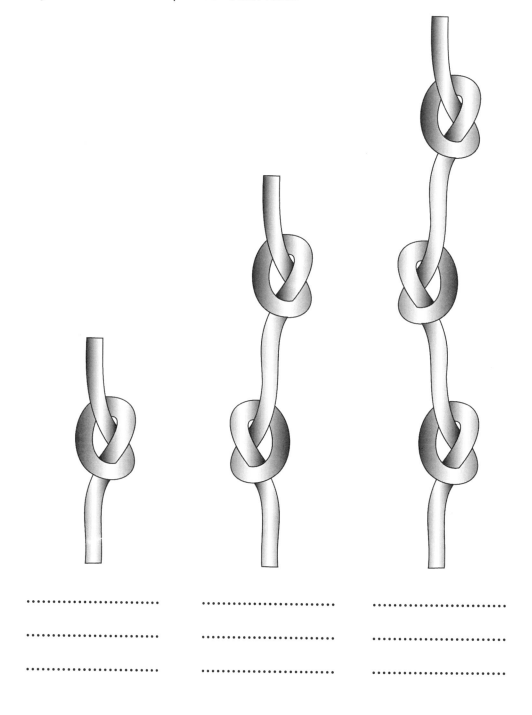

....

....

....

Exercise 4

Directions: Read each phrase and suggest Islamic phrases to replace the following phrases. Write down what you should say instead.

"Wow! The is so cool!"

_____
_____
_____
_____

"Oh! I'm so sorry!"

_____
_____
_____
_____

"Oh! need to get that evil thought out!"

_____
_____
_____
_____

"Thank you!"

_____
_____
_____
_____

"Your house is so big,"

_____
_____
_____
_____

Exercise 1

Directions:Sadaqah is not only giving money. You can do other acts of kindness as Sadaqah. In each box, draw yourself preforming one of these types of sadaqah.

Exercise 2

Directions: Complete each of the benefits of Zakah by replacing the underlined word with the correct word.

1. <u>YELP</u> others. ....

2. Build a <u>LONG</u> community. ....

3. Enter <u>HENNA</u>. ....

4. <u>DRESSES</u> our wealth. ....

Exercise 3

Directions: Divide the food produced by the garden as mentioned in the story into three parts and label where each part goes.

UNIT D

Exercise 1

Directions: Read the sentences. Follow the directions to fill in the boxes and discover the secret message.

1 - In the first row of boxes put:

- The last letter in the word prayed in the fourth box
- The first vowel in the word Makkah in the third box
- The second vowel in the word "prophet" in the second box
- The second consonant in the word "Qur'an" in the first box

☐ ☐ ☐ ☐

2 - In the second row of boxes put:

- The last consonant in the word Jama'ah in the first box
- The first vowel in the word Jibreel in the second box
- The second consonant in the word Quraysh in the third box
- The last vowel in the word Allah in the fourth box

☐ ☐ ☐ ☐

3 - In the third row of boxes put:

- The second consonant in the word tawrah in the first box
- The first letter in the word angel in the second, fourth, and sixth boxes
- The last letter in the word surah in the seventh box
- The second consonant the word prophet in the third box
- The first letter in the word Qur'an in the fifth box

☐ ☐ ☐ ☐ ☐ ☐ ☐

Exercise 2

Directions: You have to find out exact information about the "New Prophet. "Then, answer the five W's: Who? What? Where? When? Why?

The New Prophet

When did Mohammad become a prophet?

....

....

Where did he receive the prophet-hood?

....

....

Who visited him in the cave?

....

....

What were the first ayaat revealed?

....

....

How did Jibreel reveal the first ayaat to the prophet?

....

....

Exercise 3

Directions: Read each description. Then look at the facts. Write a J for Jibreel, R for Rasoolallah, and G for ghar Hira; next to each fact.

JIBREEL

Angel Jibreel is the leader of all the angels. He squeezed Muhammad three times telling him to "Read." He was sent to Prophet Mohammad to teach him the message of Islam.

RASOOLULLAH

Prophet Mohammad was very honest and kind. He was a great man. His family and friends trusted him. He was respected by his tribe Quraysh, in Makkah. He always fed the poor and helped the needy.

GHARHIRA

Ghar means "cave." Ghar Hira' was on top of a mountain where the Prophet liked to think about Allah's creation. it is located near Makkah.

FACTS

.... 1. He was respected by the tribe of Quraysh in Makkah.

.... 2. He is the leader of all the angels.

.... 3. It is a name of a cave.

.... 4. He was sent to teach the Prophet the message of Islam.

.... 5. He was an honest, kind, great, and strong man.

.... 6. It is where the Prophet used to think about Allah's creation.

Exercise 1   First Comes First **1**st

<u>Directions</u>: Match each pair by writing complete sentences on the lines below.

1. (ABU BAKR) was the first...   (SERVANT) to accept Islam

2. (KHADEEJAH) was the first...   (MAN) to accept Islam

3. (ZADI BIN HARITHAH) was the first...   (COUSIN) to accept Islam

4. (ALI) was the first...   (WOMAN) to accept Islam

1. _____

2. _____

3. _____

4. _____

Our Stars!

 ## Exercise 2

Directions: Read the "Name List" below, and write the correct names in the correct circles according to what you should say.

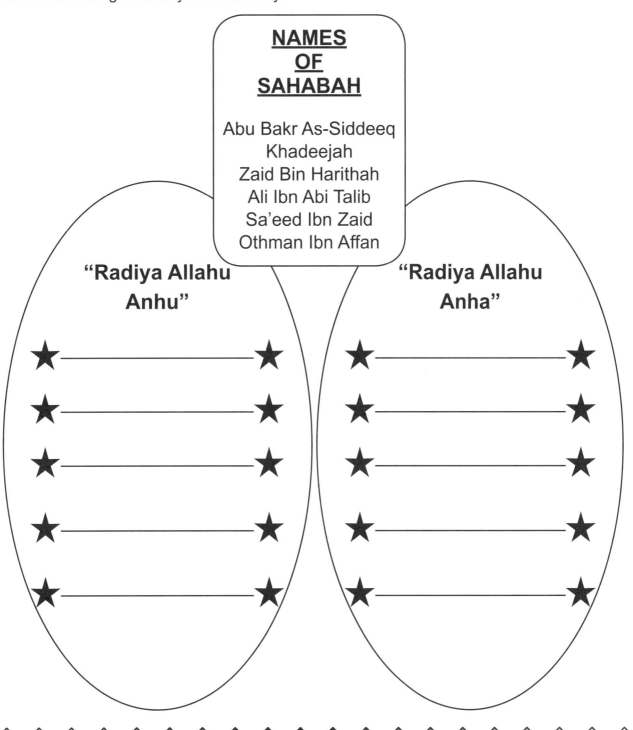

NAMES
OF
SAHABAH

Abu Bakr As-Siddeeq
Khadeejah
Zaid Bin Harithah
Ali Ibn Abi Talib
Sa'eed Ibn Zaid
Othman Ibn Affan

"Radiya Allahu Anhu"

"Radiya Allahu Anha"

Guess Who ?

Exercise 1

Directions: Read each fact, then guess who it describes. Write in the correct answer by choosing it from the word bank.

WORD BANK

Yasir	Abu Jahil	Abdullah Ibn Masoud
Sumayyah	Ammar Ibn Yasir	Abu Bakr As-Siddeeq
Bilal Ibn Rabah	Umayyah Ibn Khalaf	Hamamah

1. She was the first woman martyr to die for the sake of Allah.
   Who is she? ....

2. He was one of the greatest Sahabah. He was the first to read Qur'an in a loud voice by Al-Ka'bah.
   Who is he? ....

3. She was Bilal's mother.
   Whi is she? ....

4. His real name was Amr Ibn Hisham, but because he was an enemy of Islam, the Prophet called him "Father of Ignorance."
   Who is he? ....

5. Both his parents were killed because they refused to leave Islam and worship idols. They were the first martyrs.
   Who is he? ....

6. He was a slave in Makkah and became the Prophet's Mua'thin after he was freed.
   Who is he? ....

7. He was tortured by Abu Jahl for accepting Islam and was promised Paradise for dying the sake of Allah.
   Who is he? ....

8. He freed Bilal and his mother.
   Who is he? ....

9. He was the slave owner who would whip and torture Bilal on the hot sand.
   Who is he? ....

Exercise 2

Directions: Fill in the blanks to complete the paragraph. Then, use the letter in each shape to answer the question at the bottom.

1- People in Makkah used to worship idols and statues. They thought that worshiping these gods would bring them closer to Allah (SWT). This is called:

_____ _____ _____ ○ _____

2- Ummayah ibn Khalaf used to turture Bilal after he became muslim. Bilal was from a country in Africa called:

_____ □ _____ _____ ♡ _____ _____ _____ _____

3- These were the words repeated by Bilal when Umayyah ordered that a rock be placed on his chest.

_____ _____ △ _____

4- He was one of the greatest Sahabah who had his ear cut off by Abu Jahl for reading Qur'an by Al-Ka'bah. His name was Abdullah ibn:

_____ _____ ⌂ _____ _____

Allah Is :

_____ _____ _____ _____ _____ _____ _____ _____
△ ♡ ♡ △ □ ⌂ ⌂ ○

67

Exercise 1

Directions: Match the problem with the proper description.

1- Name calling the Prophet

> They offered to give the Prophet a lot of money and to make him their king. In return, they wanted the Prophet to stop teaching Islam to others.

2- Kill the Prophet

> They called the Prophet poet, fortune teller, and even sorcerer. People knew that the Prophet was none of these.

3- Making generous offers

> Quraysh told the Prophet that they would worship Allah (SWT) some of the time and he would have to worship their idols sometimes.

4- Making a deal

> They offered to give Abu Talib one of the best young men of Quraysh to adopt as his son in return for Muhammad.

PATIENCE TEST

Exercise 1

Directions: Number the plans in the order in which the Quraysh tried them..

☐   Making a deal

☐   Making generous offers

☐   Name calling the Prophet

☐   Kill the Prophet

Exercise 3

Directions: What would you do in the following situations?

1 ◆ Someone called you a very bad name.

----

2 ◆ Someone stole your favorite toy.

----

3 ◆ Your sister spilled juice on your homework you just completed.

----

4 ◆ You lost a basketball game.

----

5 ◆ Your mother tells you that you cannot buy the game you have been waiting for a long time.

----

6 ◆ you have to wait in a long line to go a ride.

Analogies

Exercise 4

Directions: Fill in the blanks with the proper word from the word bank.

1. Day is to night as Dunya

is to ....

WORD BANK

Akhirah
Idols
Sabr
A Poet

2. Wealth is to ثراء as patience

is to ....

3. Fortune is to rich as

poetry is to ....

4. Muslims is to Allah as Quraysh

is to ....

Guess Who?

Exercise 1

Directions: Read each fact, then guess who it describes. Write in the correct answer by choosing it from the word bank.

> **Word Bank**
>
> -Bani Hashim   -Khadeejah   -Abu Bakr
> -Abu Talib   -Uqbah ibn Abi Mu'ayt   -Fatimah

1- The daughter of the Prophet was crying because the cruel idol worshipers hurt him.
Who is she? ....

2- She was the Prophet's best friend. She gave him love and strength and was the first female Muslim. She passed away in the "year of sorrow."
Who is she? ....

3- They refused to give up Muhammad to the Quraysh. As a result, they suffered the boycott with the Muslims.
Who are they? ....

4- The Prophet's uncle that died in the "year of sorrow."
Who is he? ....

5- A chief that tried to kill the Prophet.
Who is he? ....

6- He pushed Uqbah away and yelled, "You would kill a man just because he says Allah is my God?"
Who is he? ....

 ## Exercise 2

Directions: Complete the crossword puzzle below.

ACROSS:

1. The tribe that was loyal to the Prophet and suffered with the Muslims.

4. The year that Abu Talib and Khadeeja died in was called the "year of ....".

5. He tried to kill the Prophet. His name was..................... ibn Abi Mu'yat.

7. She accepted Islam after the Prophet.

DOWN:

1. This means nobody is allowed to talk to them, marry them, buy their goods, or sell anything to them.

3. This was what they called the agreement between the chiefs. It means "the page."

6. The chiefs of this tribe were afraid that Muslims would take over Makkah.

8. He was the most cruel amongst the chiefs and supported the boycott

Exercise 3

Directions: Fill in the boycott agreement below.

BOYCOTT!

What is a boycott?

....

What is the agreement known as?

....

Who made this agreement?

....

What did it say?

....
....

What was the result?

....
....
....

ALLAH IS ...

Exercise 1

Directions: Find out if each statement is TRUE or FALSE. Write the letters to each answer in the blanks below.

	TRUE	FALSE
1. Allah سبحانه وتعالى took the Prophet (PBUH) on Al-Israawal mi'raj to teach him a lesson.	L	A
2. The Prophet rode on Al-Buraq to Al-Aqsa Mosque.	L	Y
3. Al-Aqsa Mosque is located in Madinah.	S	A
4. The journey took a month to complete.	Y	L
5. The Prophet saw a special tree in heaven. The name of that tree is Sidratul Muntaha.	I	S
6. One prayer is equal to fifty.	I	Y
7. The Prophet described the city and Al-Masjid Al-Aqsa to Abu Bakr wrong.	L	Y

_____ _____ _ _____ _____ _____ _____ _____

Exercise 2

Directions: Number the events in order. Then, write them in correct order on the lines provided.

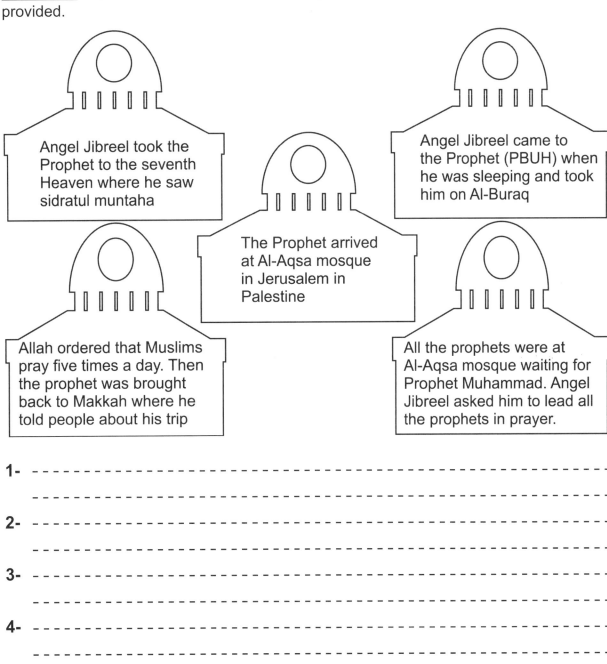

Angel Jibreel took the Prophet to the seventh Heaven where he saw sidratul muntaha

Angel Jibreel came to the Prophet (PBUH) when he was sleeping and took him on Al-Buraq

The Prophet arrived at Al-Aqsa mosque in Jerusalem in Palestine

Allah ordered that Muslims pray five times a day. Then the prophet was brought back to Makkah where he told people about his trip

All the prophets were at Al-Aqsa mosque waiting for Prophet Muhammad. Angel Jibreel asked him to lead all the prophets in prayer.

1- _____

_____

2- _____

_____

3- _____

_____

4- _____

_____

5- _____

_____

THE HEAVENLY
TRIP SCRAMBLE

✿ **Exercise 3**

Directions: Use the hints to help you unscramble the words.

__ __ __ __ __ __ __ __
L A - J A R M I
(From Jerusalem to the Heavens)

__ __ __ __ __ __ __ __
L A - I R S A A
(Joumey to Jerusalem)

__ __ __ __ __ __ __ __ __
L A M E J S U R E
(City)

__ __ __ __ __ __ __ __
L A - Q U R A B
(Horse-like Creature)

__ __ __ __ __
R J A A B
(Month)

__ __ __ __ __ __
A L - Q A A J
(Mosque)

__ __ __ __ __ __ __ __
L A - R M E A E K
(Name of Allah)

__ __ __ __ __ __ __ __ __
S A - Q D E E D S I
(The Building)

Exercise 1

Directions: Find the names of the children of Rasoolullah in the word search.

WORD BANK

Al-Qasim
Fatimah
Abdullah
Zaynab
Ruqayyah
Um-Kulthoom
Ibraheem

V	U	Z	A	Y	N	A	B	R	C
B	A	L	Q	A	S	I	M	U	X
C	A	T	W	X	L	U	V	Q	Z
M	B	Y	K	H	S	W	Y	A	R
N	D	O	T	M	T	X	Z	Y	B
Q	U	R	A	S	Q	R	A	Y	A
S	L	B	R	A	O	P	F	A	D
R	L	F	A	T	I	M	A	H	S
A	A	I	B	R	A	H	E	E	M
S	H	A	C	D	B	T	V	U	N
U	M	K	U	L	T	H	O	O	M

✿ Exercise 2

Directions: Write about Khadeejah in the lines provided. What made her so speical?

KHADEEJAH

_____

_____

_____

_____

_____

_____

_____

_____

_____

UNIT E

Exercise 1

Directions: Pretend you have $40 in the bank. Cut the bills out and divide them into how you would spend on each.

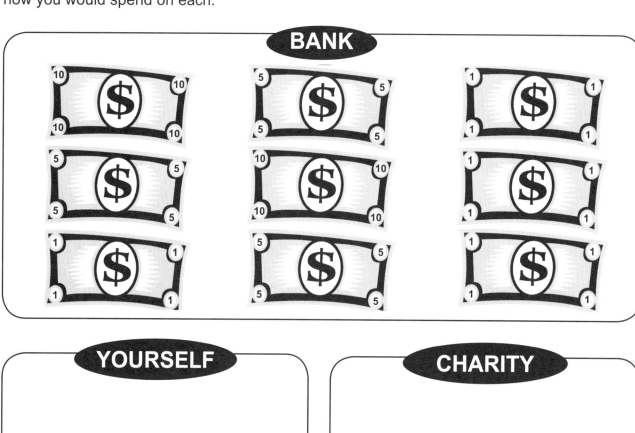

BANK

YOURSELF

CHARITY

FAMILY

Giving Zakah purifies my soul.

Exercise 2

Directions: Which ones are acts of sadaqah? Circle theones that an act of Sadaqah, and put and X on the ones that are not.

UNIT E
Chapter 2

Exercise 1

Directions: In the chapter, you read the story of the sons and their father. In the twigs below, write down 4 lessons you learned from the story.

1. ....
....
....
....

2. ....
....
....
....

3. ....
....
....
....

4. ....
....
....
....

Exercise 2

Directions: Answer the questions below by circling the correct answer to each.

1- If a new student comes to class, how do you treat him or her?
   A- Make fun of the new student
   B- Help them out and cooperate
   C- Point out their mistakes and never correct them.

2- If a player on a team Passes you the ball, you should:
   A- Share the ball with others
   B- Keep it to yourself
   C- Never pass it back to the player who passed it to you

3- A team of people shows:
   A- Unity
   B- Cooperation
   C- All of the above

Exercise 3

Directions: Use the key to complete the message below.

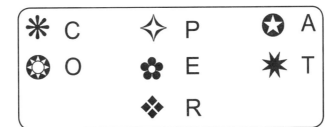

The chapter teaches us how to ....?

Exercise 1

Directions: List some ways you practice cooperation in your life.

HOME

1- ....
....
2- ....
....
3- ....
....
4- ....
....

SCHOOL

1- ....
....
2- ....
....
3- ....
....
4- ....
....

SPORTS

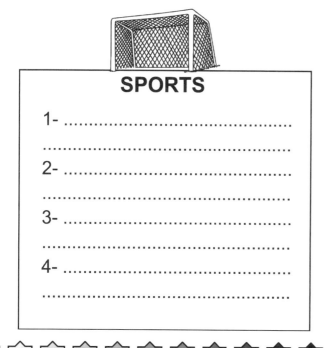

1- ....
....
2- ....
....
3- ....
....
4- ....
....

MASJID

1- ....
....
2- ....
....
3- ....
....
4- ....
....

Exercise 2

Directions: Find out if each statment is True or False. Then write the letters to the answers in the blanks below.

	Ta'awun	Not Ta'awun
1. Cleaning your room to help out at home and do your duties.	J	M
2. Refusing to clean your desk at school.	H	A
3. Talking loudly at the masjid.	J	M
4. Not giving charity.	M	A
5. Helping your friends carry their books.	A	J
6. Sharing the ball when playing a game.	H	A

'
___ ___ ___ ___ ___ ___

Exercise 1

Directions: See if you can reach the topmost house.

Finish

Start

Exercise 2

Directions: Write down some ways you and the Prophet have shown perseverance.

Some ways the Prophet (P) showed perserverance	Some ways you show perserverance
_____	_____
_____	_____
_____	_____
_____	_____
_____	_____
_____	_____
_____	_____
_____	_____
_____	_____

Exercise 3

Directions: Match the correct meaning.

What is the meaning of "Thabat?"

KINDNESS

PATIENCE

PERSERVERANCE

UNIT E
Chapter 4

Exercise 3

Directions: Circle the ones that show what achievers say, and put an X on the ones that non-acheivers say.

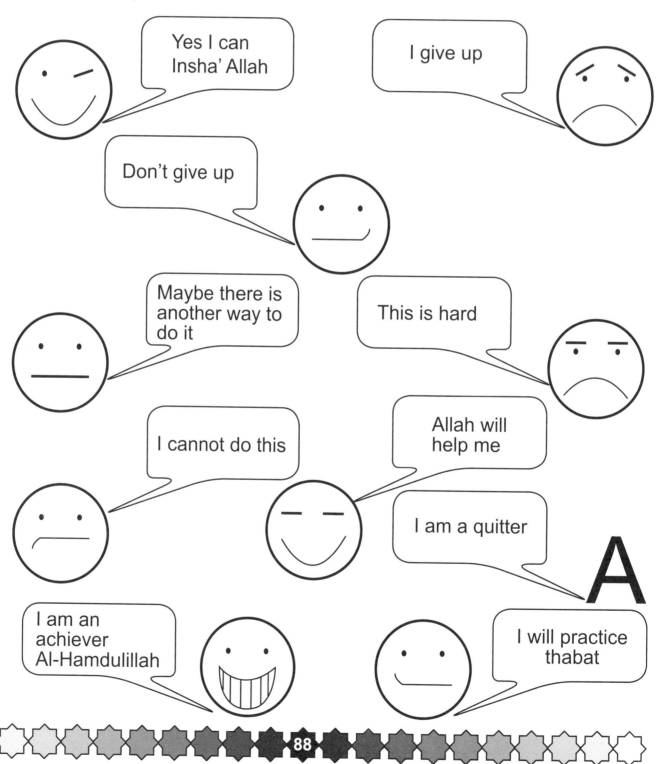

Exercise 1

Directions: Fill in the pyramid with the correct words from the word bank.

WORD BANK

Teachers
Allah
Myself
Prophet
Parents

I respect
....
by obeying
Him

I respect my
....
by following his teachings

I respect my
....
by listening to them.

I respect my
....
by doing my work and following the rules.

I show respect to
....
by obeying Allah, serving my Muslim community
and being kind to others, If I do this, Allah will be pleased
with me.

Allah Is...

Exercise 1

Directions: Find out if each statement is True or False, Then write the letters to the answers in the blanks below.

	TRUE	FALSE
1- The Prophet (P). Promised truthful Muslims a house in the middle of Jannah to those who do not lie.	A	L
2- It is ok to lie as long as you are joking.	H	L
3- Every time a person lies, a black spot is removed from his soul.	W	H
4- You can get rid of dark spots on your soul by telling the truth.	A	M
5- The Prophet was known as As-Sadiq (truthful)	Q	U
6- Telling the truth brings you close to Allah.	Q	S

- - - - - -   - - - - - -   - - - - - -   - - - - - -   - - - - - -   - - - - - -

Exercise 2

Directions: Circle the sheep that has a true statement, Put an X on the sheep that has a false statement.

 ## Exercise 1

Directions: Match the words to the proper meanings.

Assalamu Alaykum.	"If Allah Is Willing"
Alhamdu-lillah	"How Great What Allah Willed"
Mubarak	"Peace Be Upon You"
Insha Allah	"May Allah Give You Good Rewards"
Masha Allah	"In The Name Of Allah The Most Compassionate The Most Merciful"
Bismillah-ir-Rahman-ir-Raheem	"Congratulations"
Jazakum Allah Khayran	"Praise Be To Allah"

Exercise 2

Directions: Cut out the word bubbles and place them by the appropriate box.

Masha Allah

Insha Allah

Mubarak

Allhamdulillah

Assalamu Alaykum

Bismillah Arrahman Arraheem

Jazakum-Ullahu Khayran

When you meet a friend...

Before starting a test...

When we see something nice

When someone gives you a gift...

when you sneeze

When your friend gets a prize

When we plan something...